ISBN- 1523335262
ISBN- 9781523335268

In memory of Chloë Wing

The Myth of Doing

*Managing guilt, shame,
anxiety, regret and self-judgment*

Jill Spiewak Eng

Table of Contents

Notes to the Reader

1- Though I am a trained teacher in the Alexander Technique, a neuromuscular re-education that was developed by F.M. Alexander (1869-1955) for improving the way we use our bodies and our minds in the activities of everyday life, I have also founded an inquiry-based mindfulness practice called *Mindful Reality*. I first presented this body of work in my book, *Body Over Mind, a mindful reality check* in 2013, and am now furthering its development here. Thus, I would like to be clear that when I write "my work" throughout this book, I am always referring to this mindfulness practice and not the Alexander Technique.

2- In my books I purposely employ an unconventional writing style when using the word "ourself" instead of ourselves, and combinations of words such as "our body," "our mind," and "our life," instead of our bodies, our minds, and our lives, etc. I do this in order to address a collective audience in a personal manner, as this work is designed to be an educational practice.

The Issue

The Myth of Doing challenges the belief that we can do something we are not doing, or that we should not be doing something we are doing. If we really knew it was completely out of our range of power to *choose* our actions, would we more easily accept that we should always be doing what we are doing, and that we should never be doing something we are not doing?

It is *physically* impossible for us to be in control of any of our behavior, or the things that happen to us. The goal of this work is to help us internalize this knowledge so that it will automatically replace the part of our thought process that considers us to have causal power. This can eliminate the place for blame on ourself and others, reduce the pressure we feel to figure out how to live our life correctly, and make us realize that *we* cannot fix any situation unless it fixes itself. It will allow us to recognize that we cannot prevent anything we do, as actions do themselves. We will be able to see that all of the good and bad things that happen to and by us occur involuntarily.

Preface

After completing my first book, *Body Over Mind*, I was propelled into research around the findings of neurophysiologist Benjamin Libet who in 1983 discovered that a volitional signal for action shows up in the brain before a person is conscious of the intention to act. This moved me into exploring the neuroscientific studies that have evolved since his revelation. Additionally, while expressing my own awareness that our body's actions manifest regardless of the particular thoughts in our head, leaving me to conclude that all of our behavior is involuntary and completely beyond our control, I was carried into the dialogue regarding free will.

My concern for this topic at the moment is less about philosophy or reforming the criminal justice system, for example, than it is in addressing the glaring fact that many of us struggle with feelings of being wrong about how we act. The degree of relief I have acquired as a result of the confirmation that I have no choice than to act as I do, makes me want to share my insights.

Most of us fear that if we let go of the belief that we are in charge of our behavior and the events in our life we open ourself up to the potentially dangerous inability to protect ourself and our loved ones from being human. What we leave out of this scenario is that we also cannot prevent good things from happening. It is a recognition that anything we do, or that happens to us, occurs naturally. Acknowledging that our *felt* control is only an experience of effort and not a *cause* of action can release us from the inner pressures we assume necessary to live our life. Our familiar effort is only an *illusion* of power that we do not need to value or look to for guidance. This removal of pressure does not change the events in our life, as they will be what they are, but it can leave us feeling blameless, compassionate, and curious to what nature has in store.

Though my own contribution to the field of inquiry, i.e., questioning beliefs and subordinating them to reality, has been awareness based, it has been enlightening for me to encounter so many eye-opening resources in the fields of naturalism, determinism and the natural sciences. The commonalities among eastern, scientific and philosophical observations land on the ground of no self, i.e., the understanding that our sense of a *voluntary* self that makes free choices and decisions is mistaken. I personally support the phrases, "illusion of self" and "illusion of free will" because I can see that we are tricked by our own thoughts and efforts into believing we are causal agents. My interest in developing this body of work is twofold: firstly, to point out the futility in believing things that are not true, and secondly, to help those like-minded to ease their physical and mental efforts. I hope to promote compassion toward ourself and others by acknowledging that as a human race we are collectively powerless beyond the luck and resources life naturally provides.

Relevant Terms

Causal Chain: "As the universe continues through time, so the events which are effects of earlier causes become causes of later effects. This gives us the idea of a causal chain. This event, G, was caused by an earlier event, F, which in turn was caused by an earlier event, E, and so on. So any event is determined by what caused it; its causes were determined by what caused them; and so on, back through time. So any event is determined by what happened in the distant past. The entire future of the universe was causally fixed from the first moment; from that first moment on, no other set of events than what has actually happened and will happen was physically possible. This is the very strongest statement of determinism."[1]
Michael Lacewing

Determinism: "'The belief that a determinate set of conditions can only produce one possible outcome given fixed laws of nature.' Determinism is a view about causality. In its most common form, it holds, first, that every event—everything that happens or occurs—has a cause (universal causation). Second, it holds that given the total set of conditions under which the cause occurs, only one effect is possible (causal necessity). These views can plausibly claim to reflect our commonsense notion of causality, and they are strongly supported by the way natural science investigates the world."[2]
Michael Lacewing

Free Will: "Voluntary choice or decision."[3]
The Merriam-Webster Dictionary

" . . . (1) that each of us could have behaved differently than we did in the past and (2) that we are the conscious source of most of our thoughts and actions in the present."[4]
Sam Harris

"It seems to be generally agreed that the concept of free will should be understood in terms of the *power* or *ability* of agents to act otherwise than they in fact do. To deny that men have free will is to assert that what a man does do and what he *can* do coincide."[5]
Peter van Inwagen

Compatibilism: "[T]he thesis that free will is compatible with determinism."[6]
Stanford Encyclopedia of Philosophy

Incompatibilism: "[T]he truth of determinism rules out the existence of free will."[7]
Stanford Encyclopedia of Philosophy

Hard Determinism: "The incompatibilist endorsement of determinism and rejection of the free will required for moral responsibility."[8]
Derk Pereboom

"Our actions are events. Therefore, they have causes. Given the causes they have, no action is possible other than what we actually do. If we couldn't do any other action, then we do not have free will, e.g. to choose between doing different actions. The argument can be run at the level of choices as well:

our choices are events, and so have causes. Given those causes, only one choice is possible. So we are not free to choose anything other than what we actually choose."[9]
Michael Lacewing

Naturalism: "Naturalism is the understanding that there is a single, natural world as shown by science, and that we are completely included in it. Naturalism holds that everything we are and do is connected to the rest of the world and derived from conditions that precede us and surround us. Each of us is an unfolding natural process, and every aspect of that process is caused, and is a cause itself. So we are fully caused creatures, and seeing just how we are caused gives us power and control, while encouraging compassion and humility. By understanding consciousness, choice, and even our highest capacities as materially based, naturalism re-enchants the physical world, allowing us to be at home in the universe."[10]
Tom Clark

You can forget about yourself and
still know you will always do everything
you are supposed to do.

Introduction

Humans of Nature

I can only do what my body does. Conscious thoughts are not the cause of what my body does; they are comments. Because the body's actions, what we refer to as decisions, occur regardless of what we think about, we do not *make* decisions in the way we presume we do. Actions manifest; thoughts do not *cause* actions.

This awareness is a huge reversal of mind. It uproots our entire way of responding to our thought patterns that incessantly give us the feeling that we must figure out *how* to manage our life. It is not true. We only get to find out what we do the *moment* we are doing it, after we are already acting. Because of this reality, our conscious thoughts are never *behind* our actions in a cause and effect manner. If our actions happen to please our feeling of will then we assume our willful thoughts were responsible for our behavior. We assume we are causal agents.

17

If we drop out of thinking, or ignore our mind chatter, we can see that our body moves by itself around the house, in the office, everywhere we go, all throughout the day. Our activities occur *automatically*. Like everything else in nature, we are *moved* through life, as put forth by the understanding of determinism and naturalism (see definitions on pages 12 and 14).

I came upon the fields of determinism and naturalism after completing my first book, *Body Over Mind*, and then realized I was a hard determinist (see definition on pages 13-14) and a naturalist, as my work expresses conditions that fit directly into these ways of seeing life and the world. I focus on what I call our "physical reality" that I define as our continuous physical activity in coordination with the progression of the clock. This mirrors the causal chain that determinists refer to (see definition on page 12). I call my version of the causal chain the "tube," because of the way it describes our personal, seamless stream of behavior in real time. One action by our body morphs into the next, fluidly, and there is no way to interrupt this flow of physical movement.

This observation, that our actions are involuntarily executed by our body, deems us automatons. We are only our body, as everything of us is physical, comprised of the chemical, biological, and total physiological attributes that make up our material person. We consist of matter made up of molecules, atoms, and particles, no different than anything else in the universe. If quantum physics rules, then we are a manifestation of that as well.

The emphasis in my work is to help the mind recognize that our actions emerge *independently* of our will. Determinists' and naturalists' way of saying this is that we are fully caused. They profess our behavior is *necessary*, caused by unconscious events in the brain that follow the laws of physics and nature, not our desires. As Daniel Wegner (1948-2013), an eminent social psychologist pointed out, as day does not cause night, though it precedes it, something else causes both (Earth rotating around itself in relation to the sun, and whatever causes that, etc.).[11] This is the same as all the things we think we cause in our own life, or in someone else's, or that we believe someone else causes in our life; something else causes *all of it*. Human beings have no causal

19

power outside of the whole chain of physically occurring phenomena.

Many eastern practices share this perspective. Aspects of Buddhism and Hinduism place great importance on meditation, which helps people acknowledge thoughts for what they are, witness reality in action, and see the messages in thoughts as an unreliable source for understanding our life. One of my favorite quotes reflecting this sentiment is by Robert Rabbin, a contemporary self-awareness teacher and author, in his book, *The Sacred Hub*:

> We see only our own movie, and nothing we do within the movie will ever impact the situation because they are fundamentally different.[12]

Meditation can be exercised in any moment as it provides a personal opportunity to watch our life unfold *regardless* of the thoughts in our head. As we learn to untangle our mind from its thought process, our observation of reality can eliminate the place for blame and guilt (on ourself and others) aside from our anger toward, and disappointment in, life itself. If each of us is having a relationship with anything, it is with life.

In this book, I present my work alongside expressions of a selection of scientists, philosophers, neurophilosophers, eastern and western awareness educators, psychiatrists and psychologists, as I believe most of us are saying the same thing. We cannot change reality; things go the way they do and we must cope. My primary reason for emphasizing that we do not have anything to do with the things we do, or that happen to us, is so that we can *dismiss* the mental and physical efforts we assume necessary to live. Because we cannot personally influence the things we do, good or bad, we do not need to "muscle up"[13] to life, or value our mental commentary, unless it makes us feel better.

My work embraces what I call, "The Physical Reality Principle," of which I outline some basic points:

(1)   Our only tool for action is our body.

(2)   We can only access our body in the present moment, as that is where we find our physical self.

(3)   Whenever we check in with ourself, we find that our body is *already* in a state of activity/action (i.e., doing something). This state of action is our natural state of *being*, which innately encompasses some whereabouts, and an inherent activity, which is simply the relationship of our body to its environment, however we define that status ("I am *sitting* on the couch").

(4)   Because we only have one body to act with and it can never be in two places at once, the activity of our state of being is absolutely the only action *physically* possible for us in any given moment.

(5)   Following this last statement, at least for now (and it is *always* now), we can never cater to the interests of our mind when it is suggesting we should be acting differently than we are.

(6)   In terms of our past and future actions, at those times it was, and will be, *now*, and, thus, the same conditions in Number 5 pertain. This aligns with the hard

deterministic assertion that one "could not have done otherwise"[14] than one did, and that one *will never be able to* be doing otherwise than one will be doing, as the complete state of the universe is exactly how it is in any particular moment, barring any possibility of occurrence outside of what happens.[15]

Chapter I

The State of Being

Moving Our Life Forward

In the continual transformation of our body's physical activity in coordination with the progression of the clock, we can observe that the clock moves by itself. We can sense this phenomenon, the way that process truly does not demand any voluntary effort on our part, even though it feels like *we* somehow move time forward with our inner pushing. The clock changes whether we pay attention to it or not, and we are effortlessly carried into the future.

Now notice that with the ongoing changing of the clock, our body is always in some *new* activity at the new time. When we acknowledge that our body is always present, continually existing in space (whether we are aware of it or not), we can realize that the belief that it is our effort that moves us ahead in time is an illusion. The clock ticks and we are just here, *doing* something.

Let us think about the phrase, "moving our life forward," because it is partly what is behind the stress of our human experience. It implies that we are the doers, the planners, and the strategists. But the clock ticking is really a marker of the planet's rotations. As we are physically attached to Earth via gravity, we come along for these rides involuntarily, and as a result, get all our activity for free. For our immediate purposes we can say that the planet in its coordination with the solar system and the rest of the universe is the doer, as it does all the work of moving us through space and time.

Action

I define action as the body's existence in space, in any moment, in the configuration it is in, in relationship to its environment. Action is simply a person's natural state of being; it is not something *other* or *additional* to that status, as our mind imagines. So even if we feel like we are doing nothing, in reality we are always doing something: "I am sitting on the bench;" "I am eating an apple;" "I am putting groceries into the refrigerator;" "I am watching a movie." We can sense ourself through our weight and touch against the surfaces with which we are interacting (my back against the chair, my feet on the floor, my fingers on the keyboard, my hand on the phone) to get a real life check that we are *where* we are, doing what we are doing. We are always, by nature, in some place, and therefore, *intrinsically* in an activity. It is physically impossible to be alive without being in an action.

It is important to note that our state of action does not have a beginning or an end. The string of our activity is fluid, as we exist in continual time (or how we think of time). There is no break between our

27

actions, as they are just the ongoing *isness* of our body in space (as although we may disappear into our thoughts, we never *physically* disappear).

Subsequently, there is no room for us to do anything *other* than what our body is attending to in any given moment. As we need our body to act with (and we only have one), if it is presently occupied with some activity ("I am drinking a glass of water"), then it is *unavailable* for some other action in that particular moment. We must always be doing what we are doing, and we can never concurrently be doing something else. This reality is so basic, yet easily overlooked.

The Awareness Delay

What fascinates me about the fact that we are automatically in a state of activity by being alive is that whenever we check in with ourself, we find that we are *already* in some action. This means we were there, doing it, *before* we noticed it with our awareness. This indicates that we are only ever capable of perceiving the past because the instant we view something we are doing, we have already moved into the next second, and that action is history. In a nutshell, we can only witness our actions *after the fact*.

Because of this time lag, it is impossible to get behind our doings in the way we presume we can, which infers that we can never prevent anything we do, as we can never find out what we do until we have *just* done it. These conditions also signify that by the time we tune into our body (ourself), it is *too late* to retract our current action, as its occurrence is already over. This final note affirms the hard deterministic mantra that states, one "could not have done otherwise," which invalidates any kind of free will (see definition on page 13).

Michael Gazzaniga, a leading researcher in cognitive neuroscience expounded in his book, *Who's in Charge?: Free Will and the Science of the Brain*:

> When we set out to explain our actions, they are all post hoc explanations using post hoc observations with no access to nonconscious processing. . . . These explanations are all based on what makes it into our consciousness, but the reality is the actions and the feelings happen before we are consciously aware of them—and most of them are the results of nonconscious processes, which will never make it into the explanations.[16]

One Long Action

If a moment is 95 years as much as it is a second (since in reality, we cannot quantify time), then it is clear that our continual physical activity (our whole life) can be looked upon as one streaming action or *one* action. From this standpoint we may understand why it would be impossible to *impose* some outside action onto this single wave of movement. Consequently, in any given moment we can say to ourself, "I have to be doing this because I am," and then we acknowledge that condition for the next moment and the next and the next, until our life is no longer. We never have a *choice* of action because we are always just in the state of, "I have to be wherever my *body* is," whether we like our predicament or not: "I was only able to be doing that;" "I can only be doing this;" I will only be able to be doing that." If we never have a choice than to be doing what we discover our body doing, then it is evident that this *chain of action* is determined by something other than our will. Baron Paul Henri Thiry d'Holbach, an 18th century French philosopher, put it nicely:

Man's life is a line that nature commands him to describe upon the surface of the earth, without his ever being able to swerve from it, even for an instant. He is born without his own consent; his organization does in nowise depend upon himself; his ideas come to him involuntarily; his habits are in the power of those who cause him to contract them; he is unceasingly modified by causes, whether visible or concealed, over which he has no control, which necessarily regulate his mode of existence, give the hue to his way of thinking, and determine his manner of acting. He is good or bad, happy or miserable, wise or foolish, reasonable or irrational, without his will being for any thing in these various states.[17]

Being Is Action:
The False Idea of "Doing"

We have a false idea of "doing." Doing is only ever our physical activity in real time. Because we can only be in one place at a time, and there is only one of us, how can there be some doing other than our present state of action ("I am cooking dinner;" "I am eating a bagel;" "I am cleaning the bathroom;" "I am jogging")? Despite these truths, we are full of ideas about what we *should* be doing all the time. Why is there this gap of misunderstanding between the *reality* of doing and the *idea* of doing?

The truth of doing is depressing for many of us because it implies a limitation we do not like to accept. We seem to be programmed to believe we have *options* of action, which stimulates the pressure we feel to act differently than we do, or to have acted differently than we did. For better or worse, however, this limitation of action is the case, and so, for myself, I try to receive it as good news since it means we are always doing the right thing if we are always doing the only thing physically possible. In this vein, we must see our behavior as an issue of physics, biology and chemistry, not character; we do not need to take anything personally. Our actions (and everyone else's) are determined by the laws of nature, and there is nothing we can do to affect them. Albert Einstein, a renowned theoretical physicist, declared in 1929:

Everything is determined, the beginning as well as the end, by forces over which we have no control. It is determined for the insect, as well as for the star. Human beings, vegetables, or cosmic dust, we all dance to a mysterious tune, intoned in the distance by an invisible piper.[18]

In 1932, he remarked:

Human beings in their thinking, feeling and acting are not free but are as causally bound as the stars in their motions.[19]

In 1976, Richard Dawkins, a prominent evolutionary biologist and author, stated in *The Selfish Gene*:

We are survival machines—robot vehicles blindly programmed to preserve the selfish molecules known as genes. This is a truth which still fills me with astonishment.[20]

Actual Action

Much of our perceived busyness is the buzzing of thoughts in our head making us *feel* like we are acting. But actual activity is our real life in real time: "I am sitting in a chair;" "I am reading a book;" "I am talking on the phone;" "I am driving a car;" "I am eating a cracker;" "I am emailing a friend;" "I am folding laundry;" etc. Anything other than these tasks is *imagination* of action, make-believe stories. Though our actual activities may seem uneventful and displeasing to our heart of desire, they are all we have. There is truly no possibility of action other than what we spend our time doing.

Sam Harris, a leading American neuroscientist, philosopher and author, teaches that all of our activities are motivated by unconscious, neurophysiological processes in our brain. He is a hard determinist who considers free will to be an illusion. In his book, *Free Will*, he wrote:

> I generally start each day with a cup of coffee or tea—sometimes two. This morning, it was coffee (two). Why not tea? I am in no position to know. I wanted coffee more than I wanted

tea today, and I was free to have what I wanted. Did I consciously choose coffee over tea? No. The choice was made for me by events in my brain that I, as the conscious witness of my thoughts and actions, could not inspect or influence.[21]

The clock is always moving steadily and evenly, in a reliable fashion, and we can see that our body is in a *guaranteed* state of activation, productivity, and change (no matter how significant) with each stroke of time. The secondhand in its persistence moves us into the future, toward the prospect of something better happening: the next time we are going to see someone; the information we are awaiting; the clarity about a certain situation; that place we dream about that can offer us answers and solutions to our problems.

This *natural support* of time progressing is the planet in its constant movement in the solar system, which by design displays our particular choices and actions. While we spend much of our time mentally preoccupied trying to figure out how to live our life correctly, in actuality, everything is decided for us without any input on our part. Baruch Spinoza, a 17th century Dutch philosopher, stated:

In the mind there is no absolute or free will; but the mind is determined to wish this or that by a cause, which has also been determined by another cause, and this last by another cause, and so on to infinity.[22]

Though this comment reflects the fact that we are mistaken in thinking *we* have causal power to decide our actions, the positive angle of this understanding is the knowledge that anything good that happens to us (or that we do) transpires by itself. This means we can safely forfeit our attachment to the mental stress we incur in the pursuit of trying to live our life successfully. I say "attachment" because we cannot necessarily stop the feeling of stress from arising, but we do not need to take it seriously once we fully understand that it does not carry any causal weight. Harris elaborated:

So it's not that willpower isn't important or that it is destined to be undermined by biology. Willpower is itself a biological phenomenon. You can change your life, and yourself, through effort and discipline—but you have whatever capacity for effort and discipline you have in this moment, and not a scintilla more (or less). You are either lucky in this department or you aren't—and you cannot make your own luck.[23]

Chapter II

Replacing Effort with Knowledge

Causality, Determinism and the Brain

> Nothing can be *causa sui*—nothing can be the cause of itself. [24]
>
> Galen Strawson, *The Impossibility of Moral Responsibility* (1993)

Regarding the debate around free will, the philosophy of determinism tends to fall into two categories: compatabilism and incompatibilism (see definitions on page 13). Compatibilism holds that although determinism reigns, there is still a way to see that free will exists; thus, in this view, the concept of free will is *compatible* with the truth of determinism. Incompatabilism alleges that determinism by nature cancels out the possibility of free will and therefore, the two cannot coexist. This is the stance my work takes, since for me it is apparent that each of us can only find out what we do when it is already too late. This absence of choice precludes any kind of free will.

In addition to the perspective of incompatiblist determinism (and other philosophies denying the possibility of free will), leading neuroscientists and others explain that our brain does not work in the way it *feels* like it does, nullifying the claim that we freely make decisions. According to Gazzaniga:

> The brain has *millions* of local processors making important decisions. It is a highly specialized system with critical networks distributed throughout the 1,300 grams of tissue. There is no one boss in the brain. You are certainly not the boss of the brain.[25]

Patricia Churchland, a current neurophilosopher who educates on brain-based causality, affirmed in her recent book, *Touching a Nerve: The Self as Brain*:

> You do not need to know that you have a brain for the brain to operate very efficiently in getting you around the planet and seeing to your well-being. You do not have to stoke up and direct your brain; it stokes up on its own and directs you.[26]

Tom Clark, founder of the Center for Naturalism and author of *Encountering Naturalism*, expressed these sentiments:

There's nothing about us, no soul or immaterial mental agent, that transcends the astoundingly complex but ultimately materially-based process of being an evolved creature resident in a culture-transmitting society. The scientific method has quite ruthlessly undermined the explanatory need to posit any ultimately self-constructing, causally exempt, non-physical "mind-pearl" (as philosopher Daniel Dennett aptly describes it[27]) that performs mental functions such as feeling, thinking, planning and choosing. Instead, the brain and body, shaped by evolution and culture, do it all, and they do it using physically instantiated mechanisms and processes that operate quite reliably without benefit of a supervisory soul acting outside causation.[28]

Dawkins noted:

As scientists, we believe that human brains, though they may not work in the same way as man-made computers, are as surely governed by the laws of physics.[29]

Science Meets the East—Everything Does Itself

Through practical experimentation we have the results of neurophysiologist Benjamin Libet's work in 1983, which confirmed what many already believed about the non-volitional aspect of human thought and behavior.[30] In 2008, John-Dylan Haynes, a Max Planck neuroscientist, validated with fMRIs these findings to an even greater extent.[31] Science author Brandon Keim reported in WIRED in 2008:

> Haynes updated a classic experiment by the late Benjamin Libet, who showed that a brain region involved in coordinating motor activity fired a fraction of a second before test subjects chose to push a button. Later studies supported Libet's theory that subconscious activity preceded and determined conscious choice—but none found such a vast gap between a decision and the experience of making it as Haynes' study has.
>
> In the seven seconds before Haynes' test subjects chose to push a button, activity shifted in their frontopolar cortex, a brain region associated with high-level planning. Soon afterwards, activity moved to the parietal cortex, a region of sensory integration. Haynes' team monitored these shifting neural patterns using a functional MRI machine.[32]

As reported in 2008 by the Max-Planck-Gesellschaft Society, a prominent German research organization:

> In the study, participants could freely decide if they wanted to press a button with their left or right hand. They were free to make this decision whenever they wanted, but had to remember at which time they felt they had made up their mind. The aim of the experiment was to find out what happens in the brain in the period just before the person felt the decision was made. The researchers found that it was possible to predict from brain signals which option participants would take *already seven seconds* before they consciously made their decision. Normally researchers look at what happens when the decision is made, but not at what happens several seconds before. The fact that decisions can be predicted so long before they are made is an astonishing finding.[33]

I cite biologist Jerry Coyne from a 2012 article:

> Your brain and body, the vehicles that make "choices," are composed of molecules, and the arrangement of those molecules is entirely determined by your genes and your environment. Your decisions result from molecular-based electrical impulses and chemical substances transmitted from one brain cell to another. These molecules must

obey the laws of physics, so the outputs of our brain—our "choices"—are dictated by those laws. (It's possible, though improbable, that the indeterminacy of quantum physics may tweak behavior a bit, but such random effects can't be part of free will.) And deliberating about your choices in advance doesn't help matters, for that deliberation also reflects brain activity that must obey physical laws.[34]

From an eastern angle, Mark Epstein, a contemporary psychiatrist who practices psychotherapy from a Buddhist perspective, quoted the *Lankavatara Sutra* in his book, *Thoughts Without a Thinker*:

"Things are not what they seem . . . [.] Nor are they otherwise. . . . Deeds exist, but no doer can be found."[35]

According to Epstein:

This emphasis on the lack of a particular, substantive *agent* is the most distinctive aspect of traditional Buddhist psychological thought;[36] . . .

Bhagavan Sri Ramana Maharshi (1879–1950), a highly revered spiritual teacher from India, is reported to have asked someone this question:

> Why do you think that you are the doers? There lies all the trouble. It is quite absurd, as it is obvious to all that "I" does nothing, it is only the body that acts, "I" is always the witness. We so associate ourselves with our thoughts and actions that we continuously say, "I did this or that," when we did nothing at all. Concentrate on being the witness and let things take their course, they will go on anyhow, you cannot prevent them.[37]

The *knowledge* that our decisions are not a product of our will can be used as evidence to show the mind that its common thought patterns are based in false beliefs and misperceptions. These are wrapped around the concepts that we need to *think up* strategies to run our life and *drum up* energy to execute our actions. Neither of these is true. We never need to figure anything out as all of our behavior and energy comes through us involuntarily.

Stephen Hawking, an acclaimed English theoretical physicist and cosmologist, and Leonard Mlodinow, an American mathematical physicist and screenwriter, put forth in their 2010 book, *The Grand Design*:

> Do people have free will? If we have free will, where in the evolutionary tree did it develop?

45

Do blue-green algae or bacteria have free will, or is their behavior automatic and within the realm of scientific law? Is it only multicelled organisms that have free will, or only mammals? We might think that a chimpanzee is exercising free will when it chooses to chomp on a banana, or a cat when it rips up your sofa, but what about the roundworm called *Caenorhabditis elegans*—a simple creature made of only 959 cells? It probably never thinks, "That was damn tasty bacteria I got to dine on back there," yet it too has a definite preference in food and will either settle for an unattractive meal or go foraging for something better, depending on recent experience. Is that the exercise of free will?

Though we feel that we can choose what we do, our understanding of the molecular basis of biology shows that biological processes are governed by the laws of physics and chemistry and therefore are as determined as the orbits of the planets. Recent experiments in neuroscience support the view that it is our physical brain, following the known laws of science, that determines our actions, and not some agency that exists outside those laws. . . . It is hard to imagine how free will can operate if our behavior is determined by physical law, so it seems that we are no more than biological machines and that free will is just an illusion.[38]

In order to give up our dependence on mental effort, we must reliably believe that there is something else making everything happen. We have a terrible feeling that if we do not think or do a specific something, the thing we want to happen will not happen. It is true that we cannot know *what* will happen (or what we will do), but it is never correct that nothing will happen. We can relinquish our inner pushing and observe that which is automatically in process. As Julia Cameron, a current American teacher, author and playwright, encouraged in her book, *The Artist's Way*: "We must learn to let the flow manifest itself where it will—not where we *will* it."[39]

Not being able to choose what does happen to us, or what we do, is at the heart of our suffering. Stephen Levine, a contemporary American author, offered a vipassana Buddhist teaching in his book, *A Gradual Awakening*:

> Our feeling of wholeness, of fulfillment, will be present as we open to whatever's happening in the moment. We don't have to *do* anything about it. Doing is usually the desire for something to be otherwise. When we can surrender into the moment without any attachment anywhere, so that anything that arises is seen with a soft, non-judging mind, we experience our completeness.[40]

Our wants are so strong that we frequently feel disappointed and frustrated with our life. We want to be doing the things we want to be doing, or often just something that is not the thing we are doing. The fact that we are always engaged in *some* activity needs to feel substantial for us to not be overcome by our terrifying thought patterns. At times we do not even recognize that we are in action because we entertain a mental hierarchy of what is good, bad, or no action. We tend to only value that which we consider to be good action. I further reference Levine:

> Our daydreams are imaginings of getting what we want; nightmares of being blocked from what we want. The planning mind tries to assure satisfaction. Most thought is based on the satisfaction of desires. Therefore, much thought has at its root a dissatisfaction with what is. Wanting is the urge for the next moment to contain what this moment does not. When there's wanting in the mind, that moment feels incomplete. Wanting is seeking elsewhere. Completeness is being right here.[41]

Life Is the Planner:
Decisions Are Made for Us

Life makes all of our plans for us. This is a guarantee. Anything that is meant to happen will happen and everything else is *not supposed* to happen. All of the details of any event, situation or dilemma will be choreographed and orchestrated by life in their entirety, without anything left out.

When we feel powerless it is helpful to remember we *are* powerless. When good things happen we are lucky, and some of us get more luck than others. If we see, however, that what we do is always the only thing physically possible, we can *shift* our mental state into one that values the action we *are* engaged in as the real thing, the right thing, and the thing we should be doing. As our actions continue moment after moment, we can observe a very *specific* path designated for each of us with which we cannot interfere. Rabbin relayed Indian Swami Muktananda's message, a 20th century founder of the Siddha Yoga spiritual path and disciple and successor of Bhagavan Nityananda:

A subtle, creative force directs this world. As the inevitable flow of life continues day after day, this creative force goes about its work, whether we are aware of it or not. This force is not something separate from life; it is life itself—intelligent and dynamic. It is within us, too, and it directs our individual lives just as surely as it does the tides and the seasons and the orbits of planets.[42]

Sri Ramana Maharshi responded to these questions:

Q: . . . are only important events in a man's life, such as his main occupation or profession predetermined, or are trifling acts in his life, such as taking a cup of water or moving from one place in the room to another, also predetermined?

A: Yes, everything is predetermined.

Q: Then what responsibility, what free will has man?

A: What for then does the body come into existence? It is designed for doing the various things marked out for execution in this life. The whole program is chalked out.[43]

Whether we believe events are predetermined or unfolding spontaneously, we can still never know anything we are going to do until we do it. Thus, for me, both perspectives bear the same *choiceless* reality.

The Feeling of Will and
The Illusion of Effort

The sensation of effort is so familiar to us, and we are wired to believe our will is what causes our actions and many of the events in our life, that it is unfathomable to our mind that such a thing could not be true. We like the feeling of will because it makes us feel we have some control in the world. Why wouldn't we like this?

It is useful to get in touch with the experience of will by identifying it in our body as a thought that is accompanied by a physical sensation. I equate this with the feeling of effort, physical and mental, that I address in my practice as an Alexander Technique teacher. It is the familiar experience of *trying* to do something or trying to get something right. We effort up mentally and physically, and intuitively believe that if it were not for this exertion, the thing we are attempting to do would not be able to occur. This gives us the impression that we guide our actions through our willful, inner posturing.

F.M. Alexander, an Australian actor who developed the Alexander Technique between the late

19th and early 20th centuries, taught how it was possible to become aware of this feeling in our body and in our thoughts. Most simply put, it is the "fight or flight" reaction, also known as the startle reflex. This inner stiffening, or muscular contraction, is a tightening of the body upon itself, which registers internally as a mechanism of will, or self-defense. It can also read as a bracing against, or resisting of, whatever we are up against, no matter how mild or severe the object or situation. More generally, it is a manner we regularly assert in varying degrees to achieve whatever we are pursuing in the moment.

Daniel Wegner, a former Professor of Psychology at Harvard University, wrote about the feeling of will, the feeling of doing, and the sense of mental effort in his book, *The Illusion of Conscious Will*:

> Ask a fifth grader, for example, just how much effort she put into a long division problem despite very little muscle movement except for pencil pushing and the occasional exasperated sigh. She will describe the effort at great length, suggesting that there is something going on in her head that feels very much like work. All the effort that people put into reasoning and thinking does not arise merely because they are getting tired

scratching their heads. Rather, there is an experienced feeling of doing, a distinct sense of trying to do, but this doesn't seem to have a handy source we can identify.[44]

Scientists have reported that there is no explanation for this experience that has any relevance to the execution of an action other than it being an accompanying feeling. Wegner referred to the will as an epiphenomenon.[45] Additionally, we have Libet and Haynes' experiments, among others, demonstrating that a signal for action presents in the brain *before* an individual is conscious of his or her intention to act, indicating that any willful effect does not play any *initial* causal role. Despite these uncoverings, the sense that our will and our inner straining cause our actions does not go away. This deep, familiar imprint relays the conviction that we make our own decisions and that they are a product of our desires and efforts.

Gazzaniga points to a function in the left brain called the "Interpreter."[46] It is, in his words, a: " . . . module that takes all the input into the brain and builds the narrative."[47]

He explained why our biology is designed to trick us:

> The human interpreter has set us up for a fall. It has created the illusion of self and, with it, the sense we humans have agency and "freely" make decisions about our actions. . . . The interpreter provides the storyline and narrative, and we all believe we are agents acting of our own free will, making important choices. The illusion is so powerful that there is no amount of analysis that will change our sensation that we are all acting willfully and with purpose.[48]

I think it is the word "purpose" that is central here, as it implies an assumption that we must *voluntarily* assert ourself to make something happen. This is the illusion or misinformation, as our thoughts and actions manifest with or without our purposeful attitude.

Churchland contrasted how it feels when we are making a plan with what is involuntarily occurring in our brain:

> [W]hen some part of the brain "reports" on its state to another part, you experience these reports as feelings, thoughts, perceptions, or emotions. You do not experience them in terms of neurons, synapses, and

neurotransmitters. Similarly, when I am thinking about going fishing tomorrow, I am not directly aware of my thinking *as* a brain activity. . . . I am aware of it simply as *making a plan*. I do not have to tell my brain how to do any of this. The brain's business is to do it.[49]

Alexander purported that the assumed need for an assertion of will is a response pattern that is only about tension (fight or flight). He simply stated, "You translate everything, whether physical or mental or spiritual, into muscular tension."[50]

We can personally explore this awareness of tension when we momentarily *retract* our own mental and physical exertion. Look at what you are doing right now. For example, I am sitting on my couch, writing these words. If I ease up in my muscular effort everywhere in my body, including my head and neck, and pay no attention to the background hum of thoughts in my mind, I can *see* that my body is still in its activity, whatever that may be. Try this exercise. Do it a couple of times slowly with different tasks to see that your body remains in its action with or without the muscling up, or the mental commentary. Remember that action is not your felt experience of effort, but rather the activity you are actually engaged in ("I am sitting on the sofa"). This exercise reveals that it is not our will that is causing our behavior. We are just *in* our action and the supplementary, willful sensations, mental and physical, are garnishings. (Whether or not we *feel* that we decided in advance to be in that action is irrelevant because we have to be where our body is regardless of that belief.)

We can also notice that although it feels as if we need to *do something*, or actively make a decision, to transition from one task to another, that too, is an illusion, as the decision to move into one's next activity and the movement itself occur on their own. (In fact, we pass through numerous activities throughout the day without any consciousness whatsoever.)[51] We need to discount our own left-brain interpreter (our neuronal storyteller) and our muscular reactions to see that all of our behavior flows automatically.

Though Alexander's technique was developed for a different end than what this book is about, this exercise is a large part of what his teaching was about. Alexander teachers typically ask their students to identify their internal reaction to the thought of doing something. Students tend to report a "pick up" or a "postural set"[52] that seems to represent a willful, inner preparation. They are then asked to disregard or devalue that response, a practice he called "inhibition"[53] (that is, to inhibit or say no to one's habit), in order to allow the muscles and joints to release into an easeful relationship with themselves, the ground and their environment.

In my work I utilize this practice to illuminate a different point. I ask you to notice that while you are in the midst of any activity, if you inhibit (draw back on) your fight or flight tension, you may see that the willful, muscular assertion is, in and of itself, an *extra doing* that is only a coating on the thing you are actually doing. Your body is just in its basic activity (drinking a glass of water, reading the newspaper, eating a piece of candy, staring at the wall, playing the piano) with or without the underlying effort. All day long, thoughts float around in our head in a superfluous relationship to the activities with which we are engaged, while our body tenses up in anticipation of most doings. Both of these conditions mistakenly convince us that *we* are willfully causing our actions to happen. Will, the embodiment of a desire to do something, is nothing more than an effortful thought; it contains no power.

I equate this scenario with the simultaneous occurrences of blinking and swallowing, sweating and sneezing, or digesting and breathing, for example. Each of these paired functions coexist in the body, but none are connected in a cause and effect manner, as is also the case with *thinking* and *acting*. Our brain perpetually generates thoughts, and our muscles and bones continually move (act), but neither causes the other to operate. If you wait for your next physical motion to occur you can witness that some movement will arise whether you receive a corresponding willful indication of it or not. This is what is going on with our body all day long. I recognize how counterintuitive this sounds, but it is worth investigating.

I find Alexander's technique of inhibition similar to the Buddhist practice called "bare attention." It is another opportunity to see what exists *under* fight or flight. Epstein explained:

> Much of the time, it turns out, our everyday minds are in a state of reactivity. We take this for granted, we do not question our automatic

identifications with our reactions, and we experience ourselves at the mercy of an often hostile or frustrating outer world or an overwhelming or frightening inner one. With bare attention, we move from this automatic identification with our fear or frustration to a vantage point from which the fear or frustration is attended to with the same dispassionate interest as anything else.[54]

I find the following passages to also relate to the practice of inhibition; they are ways of interrupting our reaction to life, saying no to our habitual response. In the quote below, American Zen teacher and writer Melissa Myozen Blacker uses the word "Mu" to mean no:

Just No, just Mu, as a temporary skillful means, leads us to a moment, and to a life, where we exist in the world without commentary, without interpretation.[55]

She continued:

[W]e discover a world beyond thought, in which rain is only rain, not words or stories about rain. . . . This smell, this taste, this touch, sight, sound (with no description in the way), this life, in this moment, and we along with it—perfect and complete.[56]

Regarding all of these statements, if we can become aware of our mental and physical reactions, we can see that *beneath* them things exist just as they are, with no embellishments. This is what I mean when I say our actions are *still happening* under the surface of effort and will. Our body is simply occupying the space it is in, inherently engaged in some activity, with or without the pressure of our desires, judgments and fears.

Dualism/Non-Dualism

Rabbin defined dualism:

> The mind is a bundle of thoughts. Thought is always about something; in this way the mind creates the world of duality. Duality means two: subject and object, perceiver and perceived, experience and experiencer, desire and object of desire. The fundamental thought that maintains duality is "I," the subject, the experiencer, the perceiver, the one who desires.[57]

My work exemplifies a perspective of non-duality as it highlights the existence of a single actor, i.e., no *separate* subject who is acting other than one's body (no "ghost in the machine").[58] Despite the thinker "I" inside a person's mind, with all of its opinions, there is still, only, ever the actual person in the flesh who is executing an action, the individual body in its chain of physical movement from conception to death. The fact that the state of being (alive) is, by default, an action ("I am standing in the kitchen"), and the *only* action physically possible for a given moment, once it is happening, eliminates any truth to the idea that we can ever be in some state of affairs other than what we are in.

Many scientists and eastern practitioners stand together on the common ground that considers the belief in a voluntary, causal self to be an illusion of mind. Regarding the things we do, or that occur outside our personal behavior (whether it be a snow storm, a child's temper tantrum, a war, or a stock market crash), we can see that there is one reality; there is what *happens*, and not something other than that, for any given moment. This single reality connotes non-dualism.

Below I outline three different ways the word duality is used: (1) There are two parts of us, a body and a soul, or a body and a mind (causal will); (2) our felt experience of being agents of free will leads us to conclude that we are separate from the rest of the natural world because we contain causal power over nature; (3) reality can be different than it is.

(1) There are two parts of us, a body and a soul,
    or a body and a mind (causal will).
Hawking and Mlodinow spoke of Descartes:

63

Descartes . . . asserted that the human mind was something different from the physical world and did not follow its laws. In his view a person consists of two ingredients, a body and a soul. Bodies are nothing but ordinary machines, but the soul is not subject to scientific law.[59]

Tom Clark referred to Patricia Churchland's discourse in an article, "Do we have free will?" from *New Scientist*. Clark commented: "There's one sort of free will we definitely don't have, the uncaused variety, what philosophers call libertarian or contra-causal free will . . . [.]"[60] Churchland explained why the Cartesian separation is impossible:

A rigid philosophical tradition claims that no choice is free unless it is uncaused; that is, unless the "will" is exercised independently of all causal influences—in a causal vacuum. In some unexplained fashion, the will—a thing that allegedly stands aloof from brain-based causality—makes an unconstrained choice. The problem is that choices are made by brains, and brains operate causally; that is, they go from one state to the next as a function of antecedent conditions. Moreover, though brains make decisions, there is no discrete brain structure or neural network which qualifies as "the will" let alone a neural structure operating in a causal vacuum. The

64

unavoidable conclusion is that a philosophy dedicated to uncaused choice is as unrealistic as a philosophy dedicated to a flat Earth.[61]

In addition to the fact that we have a survival instinct that makes us want to protect ourself from danger, I purport that the illusion that there is a part of us that can act freely in our favor (a soul or a contra-causal will) persists because we *feel* like we are where our thoughts are instead of where our body is. We are generally distracted into fantasizing that we are not where we are in space and time (in the living room, now, for example), but instead, in the places of which we are dreaming, even if that is just the supermarket. Furthermore, I believe we assume a body and a mind (causal will or soul) separation because of the lack of *sensorial* feedback we receive from our environment, due to how our muscular tension braces us against that with which we are physically interacting (the floor, the chair, the person next to us, the sofa cushion, our clothes, etc.). Our reactionary muscle tension impedes our awareness of the contact we are making with the surfaces with which we are engaging. Touch receptors, which alert us to the *specificity* of our immediate surroundings,

65

and which make us *know* that we cannot be somewhere else (and, therefore, doing something else) because we are exactly where we are, are blocked by our continual fight or flight status.

I suspect it is our mental and physical dissociation, this feeling of non-hereness I am describing, that gives us the false impression of a body-mind divide, i.e., a sense of splitting off from our physical self (or a deluded perception that our head is not attached to the rest of our body all the time). As we are not directly "in touch," so to speak, with our environs or our physical wholeness, we rather identify with our thought process, which transmits a story about us and our life that does not take place in real time. Instead, it is based in an imaginary land where we get to be the director of our life's course, and act in the future and in the past.

Finally, and what Gazzaniga indicated with our left-brain interpreter, our inner mental recording innately bears a sense of willfulness and power that assumes an identity (commonly referred to as the ego) that believes it can act on behalf of our individual needs and wants. That makes us believe we possess free will, and that we are, thus, dualistic creatures who are not confined to the restrictions of nature.

(2) Our felt experience of being agents of free will leads us to conclude that we are separate from the rest of the natural world because we contain causal power over nature.

In his book, *The End of Faith,* Harris illuminated our relationship to nature:

> In physical terms, each of us is a system, locked in an uninterrupted exchange of matter and energy with the larger system of the earth. . . . As a physical system, you are no more independent of nature at this moment than your liver is of the rest of your body. As a collection of self-regulating and continually dividing cells, you are also continuous with your genetic precursors: your parents, their parents, and backward through tens of millions of generations—at which point your ancestors begin looking less like men and women with bad teeth and more like pond scum. It is true enough to say that, in physical terms, you are little more than an eddy in a great river of life.[62]

This knowledge need not only be experienced through an intellectual understanding. We can see that in every moment of our life we are as attached to the planet via some surface (the ground, a chair, a bed, etc.) and the air molecules around us (because of our dependency on oxygen), as our head is to our spine, and our blood is to our veins. In the same way our body parts are obligatorily connected to each other, the force of gravity interminably binds us to Earth, somewhere.

This *somewhere*, or whereabouts, is synonymous with our actions. Action is only a *description* of our relationship to our environment, the verb form of our current, physical status: "I am sitting on the bed." *Our location and physical configuration exist regardless of our mental approval.* No matter how strongly we may disagree with our momentary lot, we have no more power to alter it than does a cat, bird, mouse, fly, tree, ocean or potato to its respective circumstance. As a star or comet must be exactly where it is doing what it is doing, so must we. This interdependence with nature characterizes another aspect of non-duality.

(3) Reality can be different than it is.

The fact that it is *only* our thoughts (or someone else's) that tell us we should not act the way we do or that things in the world should not be as they are exposes the fallacy of duality because reality will always trump fantasy. It does not matter how serious or emotionally charged an issue may be. What actually happens will always supercede what we believe should happen (if they are not the same). The idea that life events can be other than they are, including our own behavior, relies solely on the illusion that we are something other than our physical body.

When we wish things to be otherwise, we presume they can change via the power of our own mind, or a collaboration between ourself and some spiritual power, the latter attained through prayer or a form of mental projection that is dependent on "us." If we did not believe ourself to have any causal influence we would just see that everything occurs by itself via some force of nature that eludes our thinker "I." We would understand, without question, that things must be exactly as they are, until they change *naturally* (no different than the weather). Since we do not possess a contra-causal will or soul that can act on our personal behalf (since the molecular underpinnings of the brain are not constructed in a way that reflects any kind of uncaused entity), this presumption of duality, that reality can be different than it is, is flawed. It is only our thinking apparatus that tricks us into believing it is so.

The Belief that *We* Are Causal Agents

We can recall things that have come into our life in order to realize that they happened *to* us; we did not cause them, or cause ourself to do them. *They just happened.* If we do not go back to our exact memory of how a situation arose, our mind may mask it with a translation that distorts the event. Our mental interpreter is masterful in this way. It assigns ownership to the things we do and the thoughts we have, even if at the time of occurrence *part* of us recognizes that something is happening without our hand. Will can apply itself to situations in retrospect of ten years or one millisecond ago in the form of, "I caused that."

Our brain creates mental images of events in our life that are self-molded to match our biases and opinions, needs we have to preserve who we want or think ourself to be. Or, sometimes we just shortcut things mentally because we have genuinely forgotten how something really came about. In either case, there is nothing we will ever do that is something we could have known for sure would happen until it did. It is for this reason that *we* can never be the cause of anything. Just as importantly, no one else can be the cause of anything he or she does, or that happens to us, as there is no human being that is immune to the circumstances of life.

Wegner explained why it *seems* that one thing causes another, and why we then assume we, too, have causal power: "People get the experience of will primarily when the idea of acting occurs to them before they act."[63]

In this case, the "idea," or feeling of will, is experienced in us as the *cause*, and the aligned outcome is somehow the proof that we caused the act to occur. This is why we believe our thoughts cause our actions. However, as we perform countless actions every day of which we are never aware (which means there was no willful sensation accompanying them), we would not hold the belief that we caused those events to occur (though we still tend to allocate our will to actions after the fact).

Wegner expressed that will cannot be " . . . a force residing in a person . . . [.]"[64] He drew attention to 18th century Scottish philosopher David Hume's understanding that this is the case because:

72

> [C]ausality is not a property inherent in objects. . . . Causation is an event. . . . In the same sense, causation can't be a property of a person's conscious intention. You . . . can only infer this from the constant relation between intention and action.[65]

He explained that although it may appear that A causes B, there is always the possibility that they are both caused by a "third variable, C,"[66] some unknown *causal process*. Regarding human action, he referred to current American philosopher John Searle, who stated, "It is always possible that something else might actually be causing the bodily movement we think the experience [of acting] is causing."[67]

Wegner offered the example that although day precedes night, it does not cause it. In this case, we understand the trick of mind because at this point in time we are grounded in the knowledge that day and night occur because of Earth's rotation around its own axis and its relationship to the sun. We know what is *actually* happening in our solar system that gives the impression that the sun rises and sets (which are terms that in fact reflect the illusion). Needless to say, we did not always know this.

This example can serve as a basis for acknowledging other situations where something seems one way to us but may be the result of a deeper, physical reality that is yet unknown, or something we are not tuning into, but of course know to be true.

Recognizing causality as an event as opposed to a force reminds us of a causal chain. We can think of a bowling ball knocking pins down as an instance where we assume the ball possesses a *force* that makes pins fall down.[68] When a ball is thrown and eventually hits pins, and then they fall, we cannot isolate the ball as a causal *agent*. Rather, it is the comprehensive, sequential series of events of someone throwing the ball (and whatever caused that to happen, and so on back in time), the ball's history, its continual relationship to the ground it rolls on, the floor's and pins' histories, the ball's impact on the pins, where exactly it hits them, what other pins they bump into before they fall, etc. It is also important to note that the *pins falling down* is not the end of that event. Though we tend to mentally isolate happenings and peel them away from the whole, in reality, one occurrence follows another infinitely and on many levels.

This connects to the way it can seem to us that we and other people are causal agents via our minds and wills, i.e., *isolated* agents causing things to happen, instead of specks of matter in a causal stream of incidents. As neuroscientists are in full swing exposing the operations of the brain, they report how its properties function as a chain of physical events that leads to what we witness as our *personal* actions.[69] Just as it took time for scientific revelations such as the spherical status of Earth, the design and workings of our solar system, and the theory of evolution to make their way into mainstream common sense, further discovery and dissemination of brain goings-on will clarify that human causal power is mythical. We may continue to learn that things are not as they appear.

I quote directly from Hume on what he called, "necessary connexion:"

> When any natural object or event is presented, it is impossible for us, by any sagacity or penetration, to discover, or even conjecture, without experience, what event will result

from it, or to carry our foresight beyond that object which is immediately present to the memory and senses. . . . But when one particular species of event has always, in all instances, been conjoined with another, we make no longer any scruple of foretelling one upon the appearance of the other, and of employing that reasoning, which can alone assure us of any matter of fact or existence. We then call the one object, *Cause;* the other, *Effect.* We suppose that there is some connexion between them; some power in the one, by which it infallibly produces the other, and operates with the greatest certainty and strongest necessity.

It appears, then, that this idea of a necessary connexion among events arises from a number of similar instances which occur of the constant conjunction of these events; nor can that idea ever be suggested by any one of these instances, surveyed in all possible lights and positions. But there is nothing in a number of instances, different from every single instance, which is supposed to be exactly similar; except only, that after a repetition of similar instances, the mind is carried by habit, upon the appearance of one event, to expect its usual attendant, and to believe that it will exist. This connexion, therefore, which we *feel* in the mind, this customary transition of the imagination from one object to its usual attendant, is the sentiment or impression from which we form the idea of power or necessary connexion.[70]

I appreciate when he said, "the mind is carried by habit," as it fits into the pattern of believing our thoughts and the stories they tell us. We can see what happens, but we cannot firmly *know* why it happened or what will happen next.

As a comical example, Byron Katie, a modern-day, western awareness educator, whose work is based in inquiry, relayed a personal story in her book, *Loving What Is*, that demonstrates the way the mind deduces certain truths as a result of its experience with "constant conjunction:"

> Once, as I walked into the ladies' room at a restaurant near my home, a woman came out of the single stall. We smiled at each other, and, as I closed the door, she began to sing and wash her hands. "What a lovely voice!" I thought. Then, as I heard her leave, I noticed that the toilet seat was dripping wet. "How could anyone be so rude?" I thought. "And how did she manage to pee all over the seat? Was she standing on it?" Then it came to me that she was a man—a transvestite, singing falsetto in the women's restroom. It crossed my mind to go after her (him) and let him know what a mess he'd made. As I cleaned the toilet seat, I thought about everything I'd say to him. Then I flushed the toilet. The water shot up out of the bowl and flooded the seat. And I just stood there laughing.[71]

In this example, we see how Katie's mind built an imaginary story from a series of mental associations stemming from one observation. I suspect many of us experience these types of scenarios quite often, stopping us for the moment in our mental track. One thing happens and we assume the next based on prior experience or "similar instances." We are sure we know how or why something happened, or what is coming next.

Finally, when people speak of their own or someone else's thought or will causing behavior, they are presuming an empowerment that implies some kind of security. But at base, will is a feeling of wanting, and even on a subjective level we know that desire does not have the power to secure or know anything, or we would all be employing that control all of the time. What would stop us? The mere fact that an unexpected interruption or life detour can occur at any time assures us that our will cannot be a cause; it is just a feeling.

The Involuntary Nature of
Human Behavior

If each person has two general lenses through which to view causality—a mechanical causality lens for objects and a mental causality lens for agents—it is possible that the mental one *blurs* what the person might otherwise see with the mechanical one. The illusion of conscious will may be a misapprehension of the mechanistic causal relations underlying our own behavior that comes from looking at ourselves by means of a mental explanatory system. We don't see our own gears turning because we're busy reading our minds.[72]

Daniel Wegner, *The Illusion of Conscious Will* (2002)

Our body moves by itself, which classifies us as automatons. This word need not scare us since we can put ourself into the same category as all other facets of nature (as opposed to only robots or machines, which we tend to associate with the word automata). We understand everything else in the universe (the ocean, moon, stars, planets, trees, bees, kangaroos, insects, plants and weather) to function on its own, according to the laws of physics and nature; we do not perceive anything other than humans to cause itself to act. We see this very clearly. How, then, could we be different? It would be helpful if we could find ways to remind ourself that we are 100% natural.

When observing photographs of humans before and after conception, we see an egg, a sperm cell, and then a zygote (a fertilized egg). While looking at the zygote and its early development as an initial mass of cells, we tend to view the new *person* through a scientific lens as something that is behaving involuntarily and not from a will. However, when the embryo's form starts to take shape as something human, we begin to consider it differently.

At the subtle point we decipher the embryo's features to be fetal, we attribute this new being to humanism, having "human" attributes, which suddenly distinguishes it from being something primarily of nature or science. We personify the body. Following, when something is deemed human, as I am describing here, it is then assumed to be a *causal* agent that possesses some extent of control. But what has really changed in terms of the source and quality of this chemical, biological being?

It is a great exercise to stare at these types of photographs in order to witness the progression of our reactions to the pictures. At what *exact* point do we switch over from seeing the cluster of cells as purely scientific to something that suddenly contains a causal will? At what instance do we grant the being power *over* nature?

When we look at art, a painting, for example, and it is abstract, we are inclined to identify something in it that makes it *about* something. When it is predominantly abstract we have a certain inner response. However, as soon as we acknowledge any part of it as figurative or representational, our mind attaches meaning to it. This meaning is what eastern practices refer to as separation or duality. It is also the same thing that happens with the interpreter module that Gazzaniga referred to; the storytelling mechanisms of our brain give meaning to the existence of the whole individual with which it is integrated, instead of acknowledging itself solely as an expression of physical matter and activity.

Whether a painting is representational or not, the reality is that it is still composed of the same chemical properties. It is paint and brushtrokes (movement by someone's body) on a piece of canvas. Similarly, without our mental story about ourself, our actions are just cells and atoms passing through various states and motions in relation to their environments.

As our state of being, which we now understand to be an action ("I am standing in the dining room"), is our birthright, and we are 100% natural, our continual, lifelong activity is handed to us automatically. Because we are natural processes, all of our behavior, no matter how willful it may feel or what kind of descriptive meaning we put on it, is still just physical movement, no different than a tree growing, a cat scratching, a worm burrowing, an ocean wave cresting or wind blowing. We don't *do* anything to make ourself act. We are simply *in action*, as when we are fertilized and when our cells begin to divide. I again cite Gazzaniga:

> We have seen that our functionality is automatic: we putter along perceiving, breathing, making blood cells, and digesting without so much as a thought about it. We also automatically behave in certain ways: we form coalitions, share our food with our children, and pull away from pain. We humans also automatically believe certain things: we believe incest is wrong and flowers

82

aren't scary. Our left-brain interpreter's narrative capability is one of the automatic processes, and it gives rise to the illusion of unity or purpose, which is a post hoc phenomenon.[73]

Acknowledging that all of our behavior is automatic, every move fully caused, can help us feel more mental and physical ease in our existence. It is possible to internalize this reality deeply enough to regard the *pressure* of will and effort as nothing but stress. It is incredibly freeing to realize that we do not have to figure out how to make any of our decisions (or anyone else's), that we personally are not the reason we do anything, and that we are always correct in everything we do (only because we have no other options).

As part of nature we are, of course, as vulnerable to impermanence as is the rest of the natural world, i.e., the fact that everything is always transforming. Noah Levine, a contemporary American Buddhist writer, spoke to this issue:

When we attach to impermanent objects— sensations, thoughts, feelings, people, places, things—we are always left with the stress and grief of loss, because everything around us is always changing; it is always being pulled beyond our reach. Our grasping, our fighting against impermanence, results in loss and the suffering that comes with trying to hold on to the constantly changing reality. It's rather like trying to play tug-of-war with a much stronger opponent: when we begin to lose, as we always will, we can choose to let go or to hold on and receive the "rope burns" of attachment.[74]

As we are not privy to the reasons why things go the way they do, or the knowledge of what is going to happen to us, what can we do but surrender to this reality? Steven Levine relayed this outlook:

We have allowed ourselves very little space for not-knowing. Very seldom do we have the wisdom not-to-know, to lay the mind open to deeper understanding. When confusion occurs in the mind, we identify with it and say we are confused: we hold onto it. Confusion arises because we fight against our not-knowing, which experiences each moment afresh without preconceptions or expectations. We are so full of ways of seeing and ideas of how things should be we leave no room for wisdom to arise.[75]

Chapter III

Using Awareness to Feel Better:
Reality Conquers Fantasy

The Power of Mental Conditioning

It is highly unnatural for us to believe that our thoughts, that tell us certain things about how we should or should not act, can be wrong, as our mental conditioning is so alive and convincing. Dismissing core beliefs is ultimately freeing, but requires diligence in laying out facts in a credible manner to our greater awareness.

Victims of Desire

It is natural to have desires, and we often enjoy the feeling of having them, hoping they will come true. If our desires are a source of discomfort however, I offer the following insight as an option out of the victimization.

Though we cannot stop having desires because they come to us on their own, as thoughts spontaneously surface in our mind, we can know that they cannot *cause* anything to happen. This means we do not have to worry about our thoughts or figure out how to manage them. Decisions reveal themselves in time via the involuntary execution of our activities.

The feeling "I" that is the subjective voice of our inner desire is only a thought, whereas the *real* person we are referring to when we think "I" is our body, for the simple reason that *it* is the entity that acts in the world. If we touch our head, face, torso, hips, legs and feet we can realize that our whole form inside our skin is the actual *me* that our thought "I" represents. No matter how intense our beliefs and feelings may be about a given situation, our body must still *always* be wherever it is, doing what it is doing. What we want to do does not always line up with what we truly do because our thinking mind is housed inside an organism that is not in charge of itself. The whole of us (the organism) is larger than the part of us (our mind) that perceives itself to be in control. I again share Baron d'Holbach:

> You will say that I feel free. This is an illusion, which may be compared to that of the fly in the fable, who, upon the pole of a heavy carriage, applauded himself for directing its course. Man, who thinks himself free, is a fly who imagines he has power to move the universe, while he is himself unknowingly carried along by it.[76]

Because our body is brought to its activities via the changing of the clock (Earth turning), our daily schedule is completely determined for us. In each moment we find ourself doing what we are doing whether we intended it or not. Our desires may or may not be met in this process, but the emotional pain we endure as a result of the assumption that we must design our life is needless. What we can know is that we will always be doing something, but there is no way to affect the choices or schedule life thrusts upon us.

What Does It Mean
To Be "Right?"

We generally consider this word to mean good but I would like to alter the interpretation to mean correct, as in that which *is*. For our purposes here what we *do* is what is "right," and that applies to all of us.

How Do I Know
What I Am Doing Is Right?

Make a list of everything you do (or did) that you believe is (or was) wrong. You can do this for the day, the month, or your entire life. We want to then put these things up against what I call the Physical Reality Principle (see end of Introduction), which reminds us that we can only do what we *are* doing in any given moment. We do this reality check to prove to our mind that what we find ourself doing is always the most correct action, because it is the only act physically available to us. *There are no exceptions to this rule* despite how disturbing our behavior may be to us or anyone else.

If we go through this exercise and give our mind a viable reason it can trust that the way we conduct our life is correct, we can begin to combat some of the emotional pain we are so accustomed to living with. As determinists say, *all* of our actions are necessary, caused by prior conditions that follow natural laws and that are part of a causal chain that goes back to the beginning of time. If we stare at our own momentary action, we can capture that it is continuous with a stream of our physical activity that trails back to our cellular beginning and through our ancestral history, and that bleeds steadily into our next and next and next and next action.

"Should" Thoughts and
the Deep Assumption that We Are Wrong

The beliefs around "should" thoughts are very strong. When our internal recording tells us we should or should not be doing something, it is attached to a system that is deeply personal and familiar to us. This is especially true if we are dealing with a cultural belief, and/or something the people we most respect or fear expect(ed) from us.

A renowned Alexander Technique teacher Tommy Thompson recently commented:

> When our name is called, i.e., when we become aware that we are being asked to respond to anything, anyone, we reach for who we think we need to be to be us rather than who we actually are or might be.[77]

If we examine our inner dialogue, we may see that alongside many of our actions sits a judgment telling us we are wrong. The thing we are doing is *not* the right thing, something *else* is the right thing. But in reality it is always the right thing, the thing we should be doing. Stephen Levine remarked:

Judging mind oversees the process of all our thoughts and actions with a constant nagging prattle. . . . When there's judgment, there is "someone" judging, there is an "I am" embroiled in the dance identified with phenomena as "me," someone quite separate from the flow, the process. All of the "yes/no's" in our life have contributed to its power, all the good/bads, all the right/wrongs, all the conflicting ideas of how things "should" be.[78]

"Should" thoughts can be painful. In referring to the Buddha's use of the word dukkah (suffering), Mark Epstein stated:

Life . . . is filled with a sense of pervasive unsatisfactoriness, stemming from at least three sources. First, physical illness and mental anguish are inescapable phenomena in our lives: old age, sickness and death clash with our wishful fantasies of immortality and therefore contribute to our sense of dissatisfaction. Second, our own likes and dislikes contribute to this sense of dukkah. Not to obtain what one desires causes dissatisfaction, being stuck with what one does not desire causes dissatisfaction, and being separated from what one cherishes causes dissatisfaction. Third . . . our own selves can feel somehow unsatisfactory to us. We are all touched by a gnawing sense of imperfection, insubstantiality, uncertainty, or unrest, and we all long for a magical resolution of that dis-ease.[79]

So it seems that our reasoning behind our self-judgment makes sense as life is innately challenging and we instinctively fight reality. But the problem is never with our behavior. The problem is that we have the wrong perspective on life. Because we do not recognize that life is naturally imperfect, impermanent, and demanding of its own agenda, when things do not go the way we hope or expect, we blame ourself, and others. We can instead see that life *must* go the way it does (because it does), and that people must act the way they do (as we are each an integral part of life). There is no individual that deserves blame for carrying out nature's design. Epstein wrote:

> The Buddha's realization of nirvana was actually a discovery of that which had been present all the time. . . . What was extinguished was only the *false view* of self. What had always been illusory was understood as such. Nothing was changed but the perspective of the observer.[80]

For me this phrase, "*false view* of self," refers to the belief that things can be different than they are and that we have the power to override reality. This is what is illusory. If our actions line up with our desires, then we are lucky, but for many of us that is often not the case. When our life clashes with what we want, what we *do* is still correct. It is only our thoughts that suggest otherwise that are not.

I am intrigued by how programmed our mind is to tell us we are wrong in the ways we act if we get no choice but to do what we do. Our wrongness feels so right! That is very interesting. If there is no possibility of behavior other than what one does, then what is the point of being burdened with this feeling? Unfortunately, we are wired to be self-doubting and self-critical. Our only option is to know it and to see it.

We must consistently remind ourself that our supposition of wrongness about ourself and others is wrong. Reality is real and, therefore, we are all always on the right track, even in light of devastating conduct. We cannot mess anything up, or make any wrong moves because we must carry out what our life prescribes. As we cannot beat what is, or what has happened (unless or until we do), we can safely acknowledge that our should thoughts are always wrong when their messages deny reality. For better or worse, things transform if and when they organically do, and that is the only way anything in our life can change.[81]

Changing the Value Placement:
The New "Should"

As our mind places the highest value on the things it believes to be true, we must determine what that truth is for ourself. With this work I am emphasizing that our mind is more at peace when it is not denying what *is* (even if it does not like that truth). The goal of this practice then is to *replace* the value placement in our mind of that which we believe we should be doing with that which we are doing (if they are not the same). Simply put, what we *are* doing needs to become the new should (the action that receives the highest value in our judging mind). For mental stability our new internal voice can sound: "I should be doing *this*," for every millisecond of our life. This is because, at least for now (and it is always now), our body must be where it is, doing exactly what it is doing. This condition eradicates any confusion over how we should be spending our time.

On the flip side, we can also help ourself understand that something that is not happening *should not* be happening. I put this issue into the category of what I call "inaction." We commonly judge ourself for being *inactive* in the ways we believe we should be active. In this case, what is imperative to recognize is that if one is supposedly inactive (regarding a certain issue), that is because he or she is being active in some *other capacity* ("I wish I were booking those plane tickets, but I am sorting the mail"). Since we have established that what we are doing is something we must be doing (once we are doing it), then in reality, the concept of inaction is nonsensical. When we feel we should be doing something we are not, we must immediately remind ourself that it would be *physically* impossible to appease that demand because our body is presently occupied with its current activity. We never need to get psychological about this. The actions we engage in are dictated by unconscious processes that we have no way of manipulating. We can just know that for each moment of our life, nature situates us *specifically* where it does and not somewhere else.

Regardless of how serious or lighthearted a matter may be, this application is the same. If I thought I should be eating well and I am not, my mind would typically classify that as a deficiency on my part. Changing the value placement means that instead of thinking, "I should be eating well," my mind can now accurately report, "I *should not* be eating well (unless or until I am)." This can be my new inner recording.

All Actions Are Equal

In terms of our doings, all of our actions are equal because they are simply a series of connected, physical movements, strung together in one flowing chain of activity. Labeling action as good or bad is attached to a hierarchy of value placements in our head. We have biases (eating vegetables is better than eating junk food, taking a walk is better than watching television, doing homework is better than playing video games, calling one's parent is better than not calling one's parent), but it is only our mental conditioning that makes us favor one thing over another. I like to tell myself that all of my actions are equal in size, as every one of them is executed by my body, which always consists of the same physical dimensions. In a collection of Buddhist writings, Shodo Harada, a modern day Zen Buddhist priest, communicated:

> When we let go of extraneous thoughts and see each thing exactly as is, with no stain of mental understanding and dualism, everything we see is true and new and beautiful. . . . No matter what is encountered, there is nothing that is not the truth. When we look at

something and don't recognize it as the truth, that is not the fault of the thing we are seeing; it is because our vision is obscured by explanations and discursive thoughts.[82]

Mindfulness

We do not associate action with physical activity; we equate it with thoughts and ideas. It is, for some illogical reason, counterintuitive for us to relate to our actions as physical; instead we sense them to be *mental* doings. I had a dance teacher who said, "Do what you think you are doing."[83] What he meant was to hone in on the activity of the dance move itself, instead of our thoughts *about* the dance move. It was a comment on mindfulness.

This is where the glitch lies in understanding the difference between reality and our general perception of how our life transpires. We *think* about our life, but our life is only our body moving through its physical activities in real time. More specifically, we think about our actions, or doing our actions, not realizing that we are *in* them when we are physically in them. Anything other than our actual doings is only an intellectual account of our life, what we call *situations*.

We can notice that instead of making decisions in the way it feels like we do, our body simply *passes* into its next action spontaneously, despite anything we are ever thinking about, because whether we are aware of ourself or not, we are always moving through the spaces we are occupying in our lifelong train of activity. Meanwhile, as soon as we are conscious of doing something, we receive a mental narrative telling us what we are doing and why we are doing it. This cerebral ritual makes us believe we consciously made a decision, when all we really did was *witness* ourself transitioning into our next physical task.

As presented earlier, it has been widely acknowledged by scientists that the volition to act in the brain is unconscious and *precedes* our conscious awareness of what we are about to do. So where we generally perceive thought to cause action (thought$\Rightarrow$action), rather, action just *is*, or we are just *in* it, while our thoughts habitually circle all of our behavior, trying to guess in advance or justify after the fact. Despite popular belief, we do not *use* our thoughts to create our actions. To accurately reflect this reality, instead of indulging our thoughts in the typical way we are accustomed (to find out how we are going to get through a day, for example), we can mindfully observe our causal chain of activity as it unfolds in real time.

The Physical Reality Test

This is an exercise I outlined very carefully in my first book, *Body Over Mind*. With this application it is helpful to notice the kinds of thoughts we have that, under the surface, are begging for some kind of action, putting pressure on us to *do* something about a situation in our life.

In this case we must apply what I call, the Physical Reality Test: 1) Find a "should" thought behind your mental stress; 2) Pare the thought down to something specific like, "I feel like I should be quitting my job;" 3) Ask yourself the question: "Is it *physically* possible for me to be doing this right now?" (If your body is engaged in some other task, then the answer is no); 4) Now tell yourself that if it is physically impossible for you to attend to that action right now (quitting your job because you are currently cleaning the bathtub), then what follows is, "I should not be quitting my job now," which subsequently means, "I am not supposed to be quitting my job now," and finally, "I am supposed to be cleaning the bathtub now." (In all of these examples it is useful to

106

remember that whenever you will be checking in with yourself, it will be now.)

Despite this reality check, your mind may continue to pull on you, doubting the legitimacy of your status. But, at least you have clarified to yourself that what your thoughts are urging you to do is not *realistically* possible, which reckons the demand delusional. Simply put, it is *never* true that we should be doing something we are not doing.

In the Face of Guilt and Desire

It is challenging to put this work up against guilt, shame, and intense desire. Sometimes thoughts are so strong we cannot get around them or even recognize them as thoughts. This is when we must get very technical about what the *implied* action is behind our stress. An example of digging for a specific action could look like this: "I feel bad. Elena makes me feel bad. I wish Elena would call me. I should tell Elena she needs to call me. I should call Elena and tell her this. I need to *pick up the phone* right now and *tell her*." I offer this series of thoughts because we are often just left with a bad feeling that, in and of itself, does not indicate an action.

If we probe our psyche, we may find a tangible activity that we believe would get at the heart of our pain. We then take this task and put it up against the Physical Reality Test. Is it physically possible right now to *pick up the phone*? That would require the use and availability of my body. However, if my body is currently engaged in another activity, then it is *unavailable* to me at this moment. (This reminds me of "occupied" signs on train restroom doors.) We really need to understand that action can *only* be executed by the body itself in the form of a physical activity (in real time), as *any* other doing is a fantasy. Remember, too, that the state of being alive is inherently a state of activity, so there is never a time when we are not engaged in some action, which means we are *indefinitely* unavailable to satisfy any other need.

This is no different than acknowledging that it is raining when we wish it were sunny. We must wait to see what condition the weather changes into just as we must wait to see what action our body *moves* into. Our only relationship to our behavior is our ability to watch what we do, in the same way we view what others do, or other occurrences in the world.

Let us go back to our exercise. Always make the task as simple as possible: "I need to pay the phone bill. I am *washing the dishes* right now, therefore, I cannot be *writing a check and sending it* as my hands are under running water maneuvering a soapy sponge around on a plate." (You can get really detail-oriented about the physicality.) Another example could be, "I wish I were visiting my friend in L.A right now. My body is in the kitchen *baking banana bread* right now and, therefore, I cannot be in the car *driving to L.A.* That is physically impossible." When we believe we should be doing something we are not doing, or should not be doing something we are doing, our mind is simply confused.

This technique is not about talking ourself out of guilt or thinking our way out of a dilemma. It is about identifying an action that *we believe* would alleviate our discomfort and then sending our awareness directly to our body to see if it is available to meet the demand. If it is not, then at least for the moment, the case is closed. We must set the mind straight that *real* action is not mental doing. It is a state of physically occupying space while interacting with our immediate environment through an exchange of weight, touch and movement. These conditions define our physical reality, which is all action ever is, and, which will always prevail over guilt, judgment and desire.

Relationships

Arthur Schopenhauer, a 19th century German philosopher, professed:

> The fate of one individual invariably fits the fate of the other and each is the hero of his own drama while simultaneously figuring in a drama foreign to him—this is something that surpasses our powers of comprehension, and can only be conceived as possible by virtue of the most wonderful pre-established harmony.[84]

Rabbin discussed characters in a movie:

> The characters think that the play is moved forward by their effort. They think that what they do and say in each scene will effect the next scene. Of course, the characters do not know that the whole movie is already written, all the experiences and outcomes already decided. They don't know that their every thought and action is scripted, their every word already encoded on the celluloid that has yet to unwind.[85]

He compared people to these characters:

> Thinking that our choices and decisions give impetus to the next scene, we energize our own drama. . . . We have to play our part. . . .

But the play is already scripted. . . .
Something in us knows this.[86]

He concluded:

Our living is no longer tense with an excessive
concern for ourself. We don't give more force
to the drama by propelling it forward.[87]

Each individual is always just moving along his or her track of activity. When we are in any relationship, our body (person) is still just travelling on *its* individual path, in coordination with the clock. This means that everyone is correct in all of his or her behavior regardless of any effect his or her actions have on another person. When relationships have "problems," the tangles and conflicts exist in our head, but *how* the rapport actually goes is a true expression of our physical reality, no different than a tornado blowing, a bee pollinating a flower, snow falling on a branch, a cat chasing a mouse, or a fly getting trapped in a spider's web.

Good Things Happen by Themselves

When good things happen to us, we must see that they happen by themselves. We do not cause good things any more than we cause bad things. Go back to a moment of true memory when something you consider good began in your life. Because our mind, in retrospect, has a tendency to make us feel like we cause events, it is useful to examine how something *really* came about. Did the phone ring and you were unexpectedly offered a job? Did an idea pop into your head (unsolicited) to make you pick up the phone and call someone about a job? Did someone you did not know appear in a room and you were drawn into a conversation with each other and seven months later you were married? Did you bump into the refrigerator and a magnet and business card fell to the floor revealing the phone number of someone you had not thought about in ages (you called her and she became a close friend for the next ten years)? Did you randomly open the newspaper to a page that advertised a service you realized would help with your current problem? Did you google something in particular only to get led to something else that changed your life in a major way? Did a good friend surprisingly tell you he or she was interested in you and you became romantically involved for the rest of your lives?

We are always just here, *suddenly* inside the things we are doing. Circumstances materialize out of nowhere. If a good thing is meant to happen we could never prevent it.

Dissociation

The psychological sensation of dissociating from oneself is central to this work. To some extent the activity of thinking is a basic form of dissociation.

Being "lost in thought" (Alexander called this "mind-wandering")[88] can make us feel like we are not here, *here* meaning the space we are physically occupying. It also makes us feel like our head is not attached to the rest of us, i.e., part of the body as a whole. I like to remind myself that my skull is a limb like any other bone in my body. Because we do not walk around *consciously* experiencing the awareness that our head is structurally coordinating with the rest of us all the way down to our feet, we traverse through our day feeling like we are in the places we are *thinking* about, instead of where we are spatially.

This is similar to the fact that we do not generally recognize that we are always resting on some surface (really falling onto, because of gravity), and involved in an intimate, physical exchange with our immediate environment (the molecules of our skin touching the molecules of the air around us, furniture we are sitting on, floor boards we are standing on, pen we are holding, water we are drinking, food we are tasting, keyboard our fingers are on, etc.) If we were constantly aware of these physical interactions, it would be difficult to dissociate.

No matter where our focus and attention are, our body is always in some particular place, doing something specific, while physically connected to itself and its environment, as a whole entity. Dissociation is a way of psychologically splitting off from ourself, and our surroundings, but as we are part of nature, it is impossible for us to physically split off from any part of our body or our environment (barring amputations). We are infinitely connected to the rest of the world through our shared chemical composition, our physically based activity, and our constant contact.

Here, Now

The reminder that we are here, now, affirms that we *cannot* simultaneously be somewhere else. The truth of our wholeness and singularity signifies that on a physical level we can only ever be in the place and activity in which we currently are, regardless of any story playing out in our head.

As we have discussed, it is our human condition to want the things we want. Without that would be like reaching for the stars when we clearly live down here on earth; our arms are simply not long enough! But when we are searching so desperately for the answers to our life, what we should do, what we will do, etc., we can know that there will be definite outcomes to our various situations, though only to be viewed when those times come. We can know nothing of the future until it is here, and we cannot go back in time to relive the past. Though thoughts can be comforting as they give us hope, they cannot secure anything. Only seeing what we do reliably shows us what we are supposed to be doing.

Our script is written for us and we cannot meddle. What is meant to be will be and only time will tell.

There must be good reasons for these age-old expressions! We hold solid visions of who we are supposed to be in the world and how other people are supposed to treat us. Though these ideas may be crystal clear in our mind, they regularly conflict with reality. Only our unique path of physical action, our *personal timeline*, discloses to us exactly how we should spend our time; it is a guarantee of occurrence. Even if it tells a story we cannot relate to, it is all that will ever be for each of us.

There is nothing we need to do but wait to be shown the complete tale of our life. In the meantime, every ounce of work we believe we must generate, even in the pursuit of waiting, is just part of the overall *illusion* of effort. None of our inner straining causes anything. Everything we do, good, bad, or otherwise, does itself through us as we observe our acting person to be part of nature in motion.

Notes

Relevant Terms

1. Michael Lacewing, "Determinism," *Routledge, Taylor & Francis Group, A Level Philosophy,* Ethics/FreeWill/Handouts/Determinism (doc), 2, accessed Sept. 12, 2015, http://www.alevelphilosophy.co.uk/resources/free-handouts-library/handouts-library/ethics/.

2. Lacewing, "Determinism," 1.

3. *The Merriam-Webster Dictionary,* accessed Oct. 9, 2015, http://www.merriam-webster.com/dictionary/free%20will.

4. Sam Harris, *Free Will* (New York: Free Press, 2012), 6.

5. Derk Pereboom, editor, *Free Will: Hackett Readings in Philosophy* (Indianapolis: Hackett Publishing Co., Inc., 2009), 217.

6. Michael McKenna and Justin D. Coates, "Compatibilism," *Stanford Encyclopedia of Philosophy* (Feb. 25, 2015), http://plato.stanford.edu/entries/compatibilism/.

7. Kadri Vihvelin, "Arguments for Incompatibilism," *Stanford Encyclopedia of Philosophy* (March 1, 2011), http://plato.stanford.edu/entries/incompatibilism-arguments/.

8. Pereboom, *Free Will*, x.

9. Lacewing, "Determinism," 3.

10. Tom Clark, "A Guide to Naturalism: Statement on Naturalism," *Center for Naturalism,* accessed Nov. 14, 2015, www.centerfornaturalism.org/descriptions.htm.

Introduction

11. Daniel M. Wegner, *The Illusion of Conscious Will* (Cambridge: The MIT Press, 2002), 66.
12. Robert Rabbin, *The Sacred Hub: Living in Your Real Self* (California: The Crossing Press, 1996), 96.
13. Rabbin, *The Sacred Hub*, 98.
14. Pereboom, *Free Will*, 213.
15. Harris, *Free Will*, 17.

Chapter I

16. Michael S. Gazzaniga, *Who's In Charge?: Free Will and the Science of the Brain* (New York: HarperCollins Publishers, 2011), 77-78.
17. "Quotes About Determinism," *Goodreads, Inc.*, accessed Jan. 4, 2014, http://www.goodreads.com/quotes/tag/determinism.
18. Ron Rattner, "Einstein's Mystical Views & Quotations on Free Will or Determinism," *Silly Sutras*, accessed Dec. 14, 2013, http://sillysutras.com/einsteins-mystical-views-quotations-on-free-will-or-determinism/.
19. Rattner, *Silly Sutras*.

20. Richard Dawkins, "Science Quotes," *Today in Science®, Today in Science History™,* Preface to the Selfish Gene (1976, 2006): xxi, accessed May 12, 2015, http://todayinsci.com/D/Dawkins_Richard/DawkinsRichard-Quotations.htm.

21. Harris, *Free Will*, 7-8.

22. Rattner, *Silly Sutras*.

23. Harris, *Free Will*, 38.

Chapter II

24. Galen Strawson, "The Impossibility of Moral Responsibility," *Springer*: *Philosophical Studies:* An International Journal for Philosophy in the Analytic Tradition Vol. 75 No. 1/2 (Aug., 1994): 5, http://www.informationphilosopher.com/solutions/philosophers/strawsong/Impossibility.pdf.

25. Gazzaniga, *Who's In Charge?* 44.

26. Patricia Churchland, *Touching a Nerve: The Self as Brain* (New York: W.W. Norton & Co., Inc., 2013), 33.

27. Daniel Dennett, *Consciousness Explained* (Boston: Little Brown & Co., 1992).

28. Tom Clark, "No Hindrance: Emulating Nature in Service to the Self: Natural laws, dependent origination and the constructed self," *Naturalism, Spirituality*, accessed Feb. 5, 2015, http://www.naturalism.org/spirituality/no-hindrance.

29. Richard Dawkins, "Let's All Stop Beating Basil's Car," *Edge*: *The World Question Center* (2006), http://edge.org/q2006/q06_9.html?hc_location=ufi.

30. Benjamin Libet, "Do We Have Free Will?" *Journal of Consciousness Studies* 6 No. 8-9 (1999): 47-57, accessed Aug. 12, 2013, http://www.centenary.edu/attachments/philosophy/aizawa/courses/intros2009/libetjcs1999.pdf.

31. Brandon Keim, "Brain Scanners Can See Your Decisions Before You Make Them," *WIRED* (April 13, 2008), http://www.wired.com/2008/04/mind-decision/.

32. Keim, "Brain Scanners Can See Your Decisions . . . " *WIRED*.

33. Max-Planck-Gesellschaft, "Unconscious decisions in the brain," *Max-Planck-Gesellschaft*: Cognitive Science, Neurosciences (April 14, 2008), https://www.mpg.de/research/unconscious-decisions-in-the-brain.

34. Jerry Coyne, "You Don't Have Free Will," *The Chronicle of Higher Education*: *The Chronicle Review* (March 18, 2012), http://chronicle.com/article/Jerry-A-Coyne/131165/.

35. Mark Epstein, *Thoughts Without a Thinker* (New York: Basic Books, 1995), 40.

36. Epstein, *Thoughts Without a Thinker*, 41.

37. Sadhu Arunachala, "A Sadhu's Reminiscences of Ramana Maharshi," *All About Vedanta*, accessed April 23, 2014, 71, https://sites.google.com/site/allaboutvedanta/pure-consciousness/ramana-maharshi.

38. Stephen Hawking and Leonard Mlodinow, *The Grand Design* (New York: Bantam Books, 2010), 31-32.

39. Julia Cameron, *The Artist's Way: A Spiritual Path to Higher Creativity* (New York: Jeremy P. Tarcher/Putnam, 1992), 92.

40. Stephen Levine, *A Gradual Awakening* (New York: Anchor Books, a Division of Random House, Inc., 1989), 53.

41. Levine, *A Gradual Awakening*, 13.

42. Rabbin, *The Sacred Hub*, 91.

43. David Godman, "Day by Day with Bhagavan," *All About Vedanta*, accessed April 23, 2014, 92, https://sites.google.com/site/allaboutvedanta/pure-consciousness/ramana-maharshi.

44. Wegner, *The Illusion of Conscious Will*, 44-45.

45. Wegner, *The Illusion of Conscious Will*, 318.

46. Gazzaniga, *Who's in Charge?*, 73.

47. Gazzaniga, *Who's in Charge?*, 73.

48. Gazzaniga, *Who's in Charge?*, 105.

49. Churchland, *Touching a Nerve*, 43.

50. Edward Maisel, compiler, *The Alexander Technique: The Essential Writings of F. Matthias Alexander* (New York: Carol Publishing Group Edition, 1995), 12.

51. Wegner, *The Illusion of Conscious Will*, 158.

52. Frank Pierce Jones, "Method for Changing Stereotyped Response Patterns by the Inhibition of Certain Postural Sets," *Institute for Psychological Research,* Tufts University, reprinted from Psychological Review Vol 72 No. 3 (May, 1965), 196.

53. Michael J. Gelb, *Body Learning: An Introduction to the Alexander Technique* (New York: Henry Holt & Co., 1994), 59-67.

54. Epstein, *Thoughts Without a Thinker*, 111.

55. Melvin McLeod and Shambhala Sun, editors, *The Best Buddhist Writing 2012* (Boston: Shambhala, 2012), 56.

56. McLeod and Shambhala Sun, *The Best Buddhist Writing*, 54-55.

57. Rabbin, *The Sacred Hub*, 49.

58. Wegner, *The Illusion of Conscious Will*, 55.

59. Hawking and Mlodinow, *The Grand Design*, 30-31.

60. Tom Clark, "Free Will Round Up: 2007 Free Will Round Up, Introduction, New Scientist," *Naturalism, Philosophy*, posted 2010, http://www.naturalism.org/philosophy/free-will/free-will-roundup.

61. Tom Clark, "Free Will Round Up, New Scientist," *Naturalism*.

62. Sam Harris, *The End of Faith* (New York: W.W. Norton & Co., Inc., 2004), 210.

63. Wegner, *The Illusion of Conscious Will*, 61.

64. Wegner, *The Illusion of Conscious Will*, 13.

65. Wegner, *The Illusion of Conscious Will*, 13.

66. Wegner, *The Illusion of Conscious Will*, 66.

67. Wegner, *The Illusion of Conscious Will*, 66.

68. Wegner, *The Illusion of Conscious Will*, 13.

69. Harris, *Free Will*, 11-12.

70. David Hume, "An Enquiry Concerning Human Understanding: Of the Idea of necessary Connexion, Part II," *Bartleby.com*, accessed Sept. 3, 2014, www.bartleby.com/37/3/10.html.

71. Byron Katie with Stephen Mitchell, *Loving What Is: Four Questions That Can Change Your Life* (New York: Three Rivers Press, 2002), 6-7.

72. Wegner, *The Illusion of Conscious Will*, 26.

73. Gazzaniga, *Who's in Charge?*, 108-109.

74. McLeod and Shambhala Sun, *The Best Buddhist Writing*, 74-75.

75. Levine, *A Gradual Awakening*, 38.

Chapter III

76. Chandler Klebs and George Ortega, "Quotes Disaffirming Free Will and Affirming Determinism by the Famous," *Exploring the Illusion of Free Will*, accessed June 4, 2014, http://www.causalconsciousness.com/Quotes%20Disaffirming%20Free%20Will%20and%20Affirming%20Determinism%20by%20the%20Famous.htm.

77. Tommy Thompson, facebook message to author, Nov. 21, 2013.

78. Levine, *A Gradual Awakening*, 43.

79. Epstein, *Thoughts Without a Thinker*, 46.

80. Epstein, *Thoughts Without a Thinker*, 83.

81. Rabbin, *The Sacred Hub,* 81.

82. McLeod and Shambhala Sun, *The Best Buddhist Writing*, 47.

83. Clay Taliaferro, Modern Dance Class, *Duke University Department of Dance*, 1993.

84. Rattner, *Silly Sutras*.

85. Rabbin, *The Sacred Hub*, 155.

86. Rabbin, *The Sacred Hub*, 155-156.

87. Rabbin, *The Sacred Hub*, 156.

88. Maisel, *The Alexander Technique*, 75-83.

Bibliography

Books

Alexander, F.M. *The Use of the Self*. London: Orion Books Ltd., 1985.

Barlow, Wilfred. *The Alexander Technique: How to use your body without stress*. Vermont: Healing Arts Press, 1990.

Cameron, Julia. *The Artist's Way: A Spiritual Path to Higher Creativity*. New York: Jeremy P. Tarcher/Putnam, 1992.

Cameron, Julia. *Walking in This World: The Practical Art of Creativity*. New York: Jeremy P. Tarcher/Penguin, 2002.

Churchland, Patricia. *Touching a Nerve*: *The Self as Brain*. New York: W.W. Norton & Co., Inc., 2013.

Conable, Barbara and William. *How to Learn the Alexander Technique*. Ohio: Andover Press, 1995.

Conable, Barbara. *What Every Musician Needs to Know about the Body*. Ohio: Andover Press, 1998.

Epstein, Mark. *Thoughts Without a Thinker*. New York: Basic Books, 1995.

Gazzaniga, Michael S. *Who's in Charge?: Free Will and the Science of the Brain*. New York: HarperCollins Publishers, 2011.

Gelb, Michael J. *Body Learning: An Introduction to the Alexander Technique*. New York: Henry Holt & Co., 1994.

Godman, David, editor. *Be As You Are: The Teachings of Sri Ramana Maharshi*. London: The Penguin Group, 1985.

Hale, Robert Beverly and Coyle, Terence. *Albinus on Anatomy*. New York: Dover Publications, Inc., 1988.

Hanh, Thich Nhat. *The Miracle of Mindfulness*. Pennsylvania: Beacon Books, 1975.

Harris, Sam. *Free Will*. New York: Free Press, 2012.

Harris, Sam. *The End of Faith*. New York: W.W. Norton & Co., Inc., 2004.

Harris, Sam. *Waking Up*. New York: Simon & Schuster, 2014.

Hawking, Stephen and Mlodinow, Leonard. *The Grand Design*. New York: Bantam Books, 2010.

Herrigel, Eugen. *Zen in the Art of Archery*. New York: Vintage Books, 1989.

Hood, Bruce. *The Self Illusion*. New York: Oxford University Press, 2012.

Jones, Frank Pierce. *Body Awareness in Action: A Study of the Alexander Technique*. New York: Schocken Books, 1979.

Kabat-Zinn, Jon. *Wherever You Go, There You Are*. New York: Hyperion, 1994.

Katie, Byron with Mitchell, Stephen. *Loving What Is: Four Questions That Can Change Your Life*. New York: Three Rivers Press, 2002.

Levine, Stephen. *A Gradual Awakening*. New York: Anchor Books, a Division of Random House, Inc., 1989.

MacDonald, Glynn. *The Complete Illustrated Guide to Alexander Technique*. New York: Barnes & Noble Books, 1998.

Maisel, Edward, compiler. *The Alexander Technique: The Essential Writings of F. Matthias Alexander*. New York: Carol Publishing Group Edition, 1995.

McLeod, Melvin and Sun, Shambhala, editors. *The Best Buddhist Writing 2012*. Boston: Shambhala, 2012.

Nilsson, Lennart. *Life*. New York: Abrams, 2006.

Pereboom, Derk, editor. *Free Will: Hackett Readings in Philosophy*. Indianapolis: Hackett Publishing Co., Inc., 2009.

Rabbin, Robert. *The Sacred Hub: Living in Your Real Self*. California: The Crossing Press, 1996.

Slattery, 'Trick. *Breaking the Illusion of Free Will*. 'Trick Slattery, 2014.

Suzuki, Shunryu. *Zen Mind, Beginner's Mind: Informal Talks on Zen Meditation Practice*. New York: John Weatherhill Inc., 1988.

Tolle, Eckhart. *Practicing the Power of Now*. California: New World Library, 1999.

Tolle, Eckhart. *The Power of Now*. California: New World Library, 1999.

Tsiaras, Alexander and Werth, Barry. *The Architecture and Design of Man and Woman: The Marvel of the Human Body Revealed*. Japan: Doubleday, 2004.

Wegner, Daniel M. *The Illusion of Conscious Will*. Cambridge: The MIT Press, 2002.

Articles and Documents

Garlick, David. *The Last Sixth Sense: A Medical Scientist Looks at the Alexander Technique*. New South Wales: University of New South Wales School of Physiology and Pharmacology (1990).

Jones, Frank Pierce. "Method for Changing Stereotyped Response Patterns by the Inhibition of Certain Postural Sets." Reprinted from *Psychological Review* Vol 72 No. 3 (May, 1965): 196-214.

Shariff, Azim F. and Vohs, Kathleen D. "The World without Free Will." *Scientific American* (June, 2014): 77-79.

Wilson, Edward O. "On Free Will." *Harper's Magazine* (Sept., 2014): 49-52.

Online Written Sources

Anil, Seth. "Can Neuroscience Explain Consciousness?" *Oxford University Press's Academic Insights for the Thinking World*. Posted Nov. 5, 2015.
http://blog.oup.com/2015/11/can-neuroscience-explain-consciousness/?utm_source=feedblitz&utm_medium=FeedBlitzRss&utm_campaign=oupblogphilosophy.

Batts, Ken. "Fully Caused: the benefits of a naturalistic understanding of behavior." *Ken Batts* (2008).
http://facts4u.com/free/Ken_Batts--Fully_Caused.pdf.

Baumeister, Roy F. "Just Exactly What Is Determinism?" *Psychology Today* (Feb. 15, 2009). http://www.psychologytoday.com/blog/cultural-animal/200902/just-exactly-what-is-determinism-0.

Clark, Tom. "Free Will Round Up: 2007 Free Will Round Up, Introduction, New Scientist." *Naturalism, Philosophy*. Posted 2010. http://www.naturalism.org/philosophy/free-will/free-will-roundup.

Clark, Tom. "No Hindrance: Emulating Nature in Service to the Self: Natural laws, dependent origination and the constructed self." *Naturalism, Spirituality*. Accessed Jan. 5, 2014. http://www.naturalism.org/spirituality/no-hindrance.

Couch, Rich. "Free Will an Illusion? Patricia S. Churchland vs. Sam Harris." *Let's Talk Books and Politics*. Posted Jan. 23, 2014. http://letstalkbooksandpolitics.blogspot.com/2014/01/free-will-illusion-patricia-s.html.

Coyne, Jerry. "Two Disparate Views on Free Will." *Why Evolution is True*. Posted July 1, 2013. https://whyevolutionistrue.wordpress.com/2013/07/01/two-disparate-views-of-free-will/?hc_location=ufi.

Coyne, Jerry. "You Don't Have Free Will." *The Chronicle of Higher Education*: *The Chronicle Review* (March 18, 2012). http://chronicle.com/article/Jerry-A-Coyne/131165/.

Drovsky, George. "Scientific Evidence that You Probably Don't Have Free Will." *Daily Explainer, i09 We Come From The Future* (Jan. 13, 2014). http://io9.com/5975778/scientific-evidence-that-you-probably-dont-have-free-will.

Gesellschaft, Max-Planck. "Unconscious decisions in the brain." *Max-Planck-Gesellschaft*: Cognitive Science, Neurosciences (April 14, 2008). https://www.mpg.de/research/unconscious-decisions-in-the-brain.

Graziano, Michael S.A. "Are We Really Conscious?" *The New York Times: Sunday Review* (Oct. 10, 2014). http://www.nytimes.com/2014/10/12/opinion/sunday/are-we-really-conscious.html?smid=fb-share&_r=0.

Keim, Brandon. "Brain Scanners Can See Your Decisions Before You Make Them." *WIRED* (April 13, 2008). http://www.wired.com/2008/04/mind-decision/.

Libet, Benjamin. "Do We Have Free Will?" *Journal of Consciousness Studies* 6 No. 8-9 (1999): 47-57. Accessed Aug. 31, 2013. http://www.centenary.edu/attachments/philosophy/aizawa/courses/intros2009/libetjcs1999.pdf.

Musser, George. "Time on the Brain: How You Are Always Living in the Past, and the Quirks of Perception." *Scientific American* (Sept. 15, 2011). http://blogs.scientificamerican.com/observations/2011/09/15/time-on-the-brain-how-you-are-always-living-in-the-past-and-other-quirks-of-perception/.

Rattner, Ron. "Einstein's Mystical Views & Quotations on Free Will or Determinism." *Silly Sutras* (March 14, 2013). http://sillysutras.com/einsteins-mystical-views-quotations-on-free-will-or-determinism/.

Siegel, Ronald. "'You' Don't Exist: Why an Enduring Self is a Delusion." *ALTERNET: Personal Health* (April 23, 2015). http://www.alternet.org/personal-health/you-dont-exist-why-enduring-self-delusion.

Strawson, Galen. "The Impossibility of Moral Responsibility." *Springer*: *Philosophical Studies:* An International Journal for Philosophy in the Analytic Tradition Vol. 75 No. 1/2 (Aug., 1994): 5-24. http://www.informationphilosopher.com/solutions/philoso phers/strawson/Impossibility.pdf.

Taft, Michael. "What Is the Self? You Are Not Who You Think You Are." *Being Human: An Interview with Thomas Metzinger* (Sept. 28, 2012). http://www.beinghuman.org/article/interview-thomas-metzinger-what-self.

Vexen, Crabtree. "The Illusion of Choice: Free Will and Determinism." *Truth, Skepticism and Belief.* Posted July 23, 2015. http://www.humantruth.info/free_will.html.

Wallace, Alan B. "A Buddhist View of Free Will: Beyond Determinism and Indeterminism." *Journal of Consciousness Studies* 18 No. 3-4 (2011): 217-33. http://www.alanwallace.org/buddhistviewoffreewill.pdf.

Wicks, Robert. "Arthur Schopenhauer." *Stanford Encyclopedia of Philosophy* (2011). http://plato.stanford.edu/entries/schopenhauer/.

Youtube Videos

Blackmore, Susan. "Free Will is an Illusion." *Rimantas Vancys: An Interview with Susan Blackmore about Free Will in Humans* (May 23, 2013). https://www.youtube.com/watch?v=hMwjCv2wqAA.

Churchland, Patricia. "An Interview with Patricia Churchland. *NPR: On Point with Tom Ashbrook* (April 19, 2014). https://www.youtube.com/watch?v=0V7QrxEAbLM.

Churchland, Patricia. "Free Will or Self-Control?" *Copernicus Center for Interdisciplinary Studies* (Oct. 6, 2014).
https://www.youtube.com/watch?v=pPSg2-8VVBc.

Coyne, Jerry. "You Don't Have Free Will." *Imagine (INR5): No Religion 5 in Vancouver: Bill J. Castleman* (July 7, 2015). https://www.youtube.com/watch?v=Ca7i-D4ddaw.

Dawkins, Richard and Harris, Sam. "Sam Harris and Richard Dawkins discuss: Who Says Science Has Nothing to Say About Morality?" *Richard Dawkins Foundation for Reasons and Science* (May 4, 2011).
https://www.youtube.com/watch?v=Mm2Jrr0tRXk.

Gazzaniga, Michael. "How Free Is Your Will?" *Imagine Science Films, My Mind's Eye: A Series of Video Interviews on Mind and Brain, Epis. 2* (June 30, 2014).
https://www.youtube.com/watch?v=uo_4w9JD-eQ.

Gazzaniga, Michael. "The Interpreter." *Gifford Lectures at Univ. of Edinburgh with Prof. Michael Gazzaniga: Series 3* (Oct. 19, 2009).
https://www.youtube.com/watch?v=mJKloz2vwlc.

Gazzaniga, Michael. "Your Storytelling Brain." *Big Think* (Jan. 17, 2012).
https://www.youtube.com/watch?v=3k6P5JiNzrk.

Harris, Sam. "It Is Always Now." *Smart Documentary* (March 12, 2015).
https://www.youtube.com/watch?v=NH3-SfXLX5k.

Harris, Sam. "Science Can Answer Moral Questions." *TED2010* (Feb., 2010).
http://www.ted.com/talks/sam_harris_science_can_show_what_s_right?language=en#t-1099639.

Katie, Byron. "The Story of the ONE." *Interview by Iain McNay* (June 21, 2012). https://www.youtube.com/watch?x-yt-ts=1421828030&x-yt-cl=84411374&v=0F-QpYtCW0Q.

Metzinger, Thomas. "The Transparent Avatar in Your Brain." *TEDxBarcelona* (July 23, 2013). https://www.youtube.com/watch?v=5ZsDDseI5QI.

Strawson, Galen. "Mysteries of Free Will: Closer to Truth." *Galen Orwell* (July 2, 2015). https://www.youtube.com/watch?v=KV5_bHwaUBM.

Acknowledgments

I thank the following people for their support, encouragement and inspiration during the production of this book: Katherine West, Ron Botting, Maria Tzianabos, Jessica Lockhart, Carl Rudman, Jason Ames, Tom Clark, Willie McElroy, Mary Tracy, Susannah Sanfilippo, Christopher Miller, Maxine Sclar, Lauren Como, Deirdre Sulka-Meister, Eva Rose Goetz, Nancy Spiewak DePalo, Melissa Luckman Keller and Michael, Maya, and Kobi Eng.

About the Author

Jill Spiewak Eng has been a certified teacher of the Alexander Technique under Alexander Technique International (ATI) since 1998. She has taught privately in NYC and Portland, ME, as well as in a number of health care centers and colleges throughout southern ME. Jill has been a professional modern dancer since 1989, and has performed, taught and choreographed extensively throughout Boston, NC, NYC and Maine. She holds a combined Masters degree in International Relations and Communications, has spent time in Israel, Europe and Latin America, and has worked in the field of International Development. Jill is also experienced in meditation, contact improvisation and parenting, and is the author of *Body Over Mind, a mindful reality check.*

82953676R00083

Made in the USA
Middletown, DE
07 August 2018